# the kingdom is backwards

# Notes:

# the kingdom experiment

A Community Practice on Intentional Living

Bruce Nuffer / Liz Perry / Rachel McPherson / Brooklyn Lindsey

## YOUTH EDITION

the **HOUSE** studio

**The House Studio**, Kansas City, Missouri

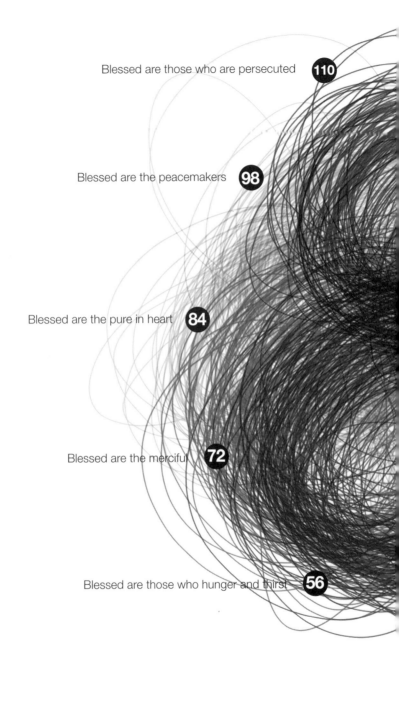

Blessed are those who are persecuted **110**

Blessed are the peacemakers **98**

Blessed are the pure in heart **84**

Blessed are the merciful **72**

Blessed are those who hunger and thirst **56**

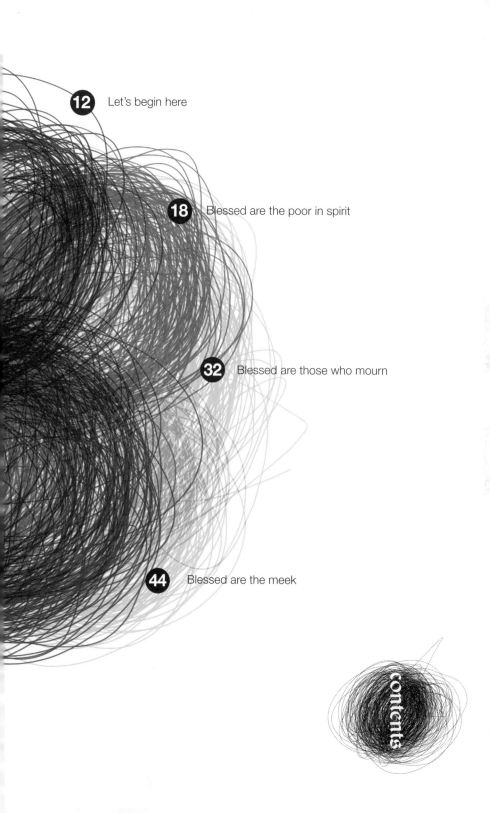

contents

most good things
have been said far
too many times
and just need to be
lived.

**Shane Claiborne**

# So NOT an Introduction

We've gotta be honest. When we started writing a book on the Beatitudes, a few of us got nervous about the viability of the whole project. Sort of ran for the hills. Fortunately, there's nothing but flatlands here in the Midwest, so we didn't get very far before the Holy Spirit and our coworkers found us.

Mainly, we just had a lot of questions. The first? Would there be anything new to say? Anything that wasn't cliché or hadn't been preached in a thousand sermons already?

One thing was certain; we didn't want this to end up as a "how-to" for getting blessed. We think this world has enough self-help books in Barnes and Noble to keep us more than occupied for the next century. Agreed?

So, we began brainstorming this project the only way we knew how. We sat down at a table and started talking ideals, what we personally wanted out of a small group. Bruce, the real adventurous servant, wanted a small group that was hands-on. Active in the community and such. Rachel, the deep, ministry-minded one, cared more about learning new things from the Bible and being intentional with Scripture. And Liz, the abstract art lover, just wanted to journal during the week and share thoughts with her friends.

Then it dawned on us. (We love it when this happens.)

Why can't we do them all? In one book?

Some will call it impossible. But we'll call it uncurriculum. Or better yet,

# the kingdom experiment.

# And he began to teach them, saying:

"You're blessed when you're at the end of your rope. With less of you there is more of God and his rule.

You're blessed when you feel you've lost what is most dear to you. Only then can you be embraced by the One most dear to you.

You're blessed when you're content with just who you are—no more, no less. That's the moment you find yourselves proud owners of everything that can't be bought.

You're blessed when you've worked up a good appetite for God. He's food and drink in the best meal you'll ever eat.

You're blessed when you care. At the moment of being 'care-full,' you find yourselves cared for.

You're blessed when you get your inside world—your mind and heart— put right. Then you can see God in the outside world.

You're blessed when you can show people how to cooperate instead of compete or fight. That's when you discover who you really are, and your place in God's family.

You're blessed when your commitment to God provokes persecution. The persecution drives you even deeper into God's kingdom."

# Matthew 5:3-10 (TM)

"Blessed are the poor in spirit, for theirs is the kingdom of heaven.

Blessed are those who mourn, for they will be comforted.

Blessed are the meek, for they will inherit the earth.

Blessed are those who hunger and thirst for righteousness, for they will be filled.

Blessed are the merciful, for they will be shown mercy.

Blessed are the pure in heart, for they will see God.

Blessed are the peacemakers, for they will be called sons of God.

Blessed are those who are persecuted because of righteousness, for theirs is the kingdom of heaven."

# Matthew 5:3-10

Let's
begin
here

We know you hate directions. But you can always tear this page out and find your own way through the book.

# It's plain and simple.

1  Read and discuss a chapter.

2  Each person can choose one of seven experiments to carry out.

3  Talk about the experiment you'll do together as a group. (One or more options will be given for you or you can make one up together.)

4  Journal your thoughts on our pages. (Why else would we give you so much white space?)

5  Share your journey.
Tweet your experience: twitter.com/KEyouth.
Text your youth leader or best friend when you get a glimpse of the kingdom. Pray for God to show you his kingdom this week.

6  Share your stories with the group next week and talk about what changes you may make in your life as a result of what you experienced.

The point of *The Kingdom Experiment* is on-purpose living. To work things out in community. To share life and stories while we're at it. To think about what good news could mean in our time. We'd love to know that once you're done with this book, it would become natural for you to see that God is doing something different in the world right now, that God is slowly putting things back together, the way they were meant to be from the very beginning. And if this book helps you turn this way of living into a habit, we wouldn't complain about that either.

The eight Beatitudes, or blessings, are given by Jesus in one of his most famous teachings. They aren't catchphrases or a "top eight" list to happiness meant to stand alone . . . so memorizing them or listing them as your favorite verses on Facebook doesn't really make you a good Christian. They are meant to be lived, and they are meant to be shared.

By opening his message with upside-down statements, Jesus was creating some tension he resolved throughout the rest of his teaching. That's why we can—and should—look at the whole passage as a way to see what the Beatitudes look like when they are lived out. It might give us a more complete picture of kingdom living.

Things to think about:

This particular sermon mattered for some reason. Both Matthew and Luke chose to write it down, though it's believed that Jesus would have given hundreds of similar messages during his three-year ministry. Judging by its length, this was no small hand cramp.

Also, the folks who were listening would have understood the significance of *how* and *where* Jesus delivered this sermon. You see, Jesus was constantly fulfilling the predictions of Old Testament writings, which is why the Pharisees could never quite write him off.

Here's a glimpse into the hearts of the people listening for the first time: Israel's entire existence is shaped around one epic event–their evacuation out of Egypt. While in the desert, the prophet Moses climbed up a mountain and received a word from God. He called it the law, which represented ways they could please God and learn about his heart.

The chance to know this previously otherworldly God got them real excited. For like a minute. And then they spent the rest of their lives breaking all the laws and trying to clean up after themselves.

This started a vicious cycle of elected priests who went around policing the Ten Commandments (and some of their own laws) with the belief that if all of Israel could go one day without sinning, God would come to earth in the form of a king . . . flowing robe, long gray beard, and lots of VIP passes to give out. Right?

Wrong.

Israel's attempt at perfection is unsuccessful to say the least.

Fast–forward a good thousand years, give or take some change. Now Jesus climbs up a different mountain and says he has an updated word from God. Mainly, that he is the new word. A living, human form of God's new law.

He even proclaims, "You have heard that the law of Moses says . . . But I say" (Matt. 5:21-22, NLT).

Like we said, Old Testament predictions fulfilled. Only this isn't the kind of Savior everyone has been dreaming up.

Right away Jesus begins asking the people to repent, which really just means to rethink, to change . . . everything. He says there is a different kingdom at hand and that this kingdom will be opposite from everything they've known. Which gets them awfully excited, considering their current economic, social, and spiritual conditions are pretty crummy.

Jesus' main intention for speaking a blessing over the insignificant was to assign them worth in a way no one had before. He was flipping things upside down. Establishing his kingdom in the margins. More than that, he was entering into a covenant with the people—promising to actively fulfill that declaration of blessing in their lives.

Often when we read the Beatitudes outside of the full story, we turn them into conditional statements. *If I want God's blessing, then I better seek after persecution or petition tragedy.* But that's missing the point. These blessings aren't necessarily mandates but rather natural effects of kingdom living.

There's something else we've got to know. What's the deal with the two separate, slightly differing memories of this sermon?

Couldn't Matthew and Luke have compared notes or something? What we mean is that Luke is short and to the point, always including woes that make us kind of sad. He also concentrates heavily on physical trials. Matthew, on the other hand, leaves out the woes and seems to embrace spiritual trials along with the physical kind.

Like authors these days, each had a unique purpose for his message. Something specific he was trying to get across. Matthew wanted to give people a picture of the new kingdom—the good things God was up to. Luke was more concerned with showing people the problems with the old kingdom and the things Christ came to alleviate.

Regardless of the writers' differences, the message is the same. The kingdom has come. It's *already* here because Jesus brought it with him.

But it's *not yet* complete until he returns to perfect it. It's the kingdom of the *already* and the *not yet*. Which is where we live—between the two places. And it can be a messy place.

There are a lot of poor people around us. Well, maybe not around us. Because in a day of a booming middle class and shiny plastic things that spend like cash, it seems really easy to forget that there are people with needs all around us—or that we have needs ourselves.

Regardless of how close we are to poverty, it exists. Jesus said so himself. "The poor you will always have with you" (Matt. 26:11a). Even for those of us who have never needed much, we're pretty familiar with what it looks like.

Notice that Luke's and Matthew's stories of the Sermon on the Mount read a little differently where this verse is concerned. While Luke believes Jesus is addressing physical poverty (Luke 6:20), Matthew goes a bit deeper. He thinks Jesus is also talking about our spiritual desperation during times of trial—about moments when we realize that depending on God reveals hope and Christ's rule in our hearts.

Look at it this way. When everything is going well, we're content to focus on what is immediately before us. But when life is without options outside of God's grace, we are forced to engage in the story of hope. And hope, by its very nature, has a way of bringing us into humble relationship with Christ, the leader of the kingdom.

Jesus was saying that when we get to a place of dependency, we're fortunate because it's the dedicated trust sustained through poverty and trials that produces blessedness in us.

Now skip ahead to the part where Jesus explains what trust looks like in the face of poverty (Matt. 6:1-4, 19-34). Most people in the ancient world lived on the edge of death—food, clothing, and shelter were all they needed. We understand they spent most of their time worrying about these things. So for them, as well as for us, the first step in overcoming worry is to recognize that a devout trust in God is more important than our basic needs.

i want you to be concerned about your next door neighbor. do you **know** your next door neighbor?

**Mother Teresa**

Talk

Compare a time when everything was going great in your life (a time when you didn't have many worries and you were very happy) to a time when you were "at the end of your rope" or had a major need. Which scenario drew you closer to God? In which scenario did you find yourself trusting God more?

In a society where we define *need* as the newest iPod, it is easy to overlook the fact that we are blessed to have food on our tables. Society has adopted the mentality that the basics are owed to us. How can we adjust this mentality and live a life dependent on God for even our most basic needs?

# Shut your pie hole.

Fast from food for a period of time as a way of making yourself aware of its physical and emotional ownership over you. Think about how important food is to us; then reflect on Christ's suggestion that life is more important than food.

**Journal your thoughts here.**

# Ten items or ~~less~~ more.

Not everyone has the luxury of choosing between steak and grilled chicken. Skip a meal or use some allowance to go grocery shopping; then donate everything to the local food pantry. Try to buy things you would like, not just the cheapest stuff on the shelf.

**Journal your thoughts here.**

# Don't even give me the evil eye.

The Bible describes a person who chases after material goods as having an evil eye.[1] So when Jesus speaks of a person with good eyes (Matt. 6), he is talking about someone who is generous and not solely concerned with his or her own needs. Try being generous this week. Instead of spending your extra cash on new clothes or music, spend it on a friend who doesn't have as much as you. Even better, don't let them find out it was you!

**Journal your thoughts here.**

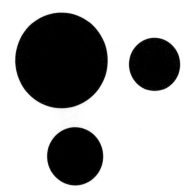

# Roughing it.
# Air mattress not included.

Sleep on the floor for a week. Think about how life might be different if you didn't have a comfy home. If you're feeling extra adventurous, take a few showers without warm water. Remember, with less of you, there is more room for God.

**Journal your thoughts here.**

# Let it go.

Take a trip through your room and find something valuable, something you depend on, something you feel you can't do without. Practice what it means to depend on God by giving it away and not replacing it. Have a conversation with one or both of your parents before you do this experiment. Talk about what it means to you to give away something of great value, knowing you are not going to replace it for a while.

# Because she believed her life counted.

Go to alexslemonade.org and give a donation to help fund cancer research for dying children. Those who are sick often see God's kingdom much differently than we do. Remember the lesson Alex's life can teach us as you save up for this worthy cause.

**Journal your thoughts here.**

# Thanks but no thanks, Mr. Edison.

Minimize your use of electricity (e.g., candlelight instead of 60 watts, books instead of TV, line dry instead of tumble dry). Talk with your parents about donating the difference in your electricity bill to your electric company's poverty account or about making this a way of life for the long run.

**Journal your thoughts here.**

# Community options.

**1** Watch Alex's story together at alexslemonade.org.
Set up a lemonade stand in her memory and donate
the collections to cancer research.  Fill out the
donation form online and donate the money in
memory of someone in your life who shares the same
passion Alex does. It could be a church member, a
friend, a leader who has made a difference in your life,
etc.  Alex knew what it meant to be poor in spirit, and
because of this knowledge she was able to change
the world. So can you.

**2** Talk to your church or school about having an
electricity fast for a week. Ask all teachers, pastors,
and leaders to unplug everything not being used. Use
candles when possible.

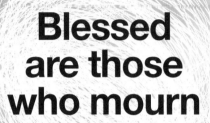

# Blessed are those who mourn

"Blessed are those who mourn, for they will be comforted" (Matt. 5:4).

Pretty straightforward, right? Well, maybe. Many people share powerful experiences of meeting God during some of their darkest hours. It seems no one is exempt from the good times and the bad times, so we recognize the sacred seasons of both grief and comfort.

But for the Israelites, a people known by their exile, loss was a loaded word—spiritually, economically, and physically. Because they were always subject to foreign rule, suffering was a far more cultural and communal demonstration. We're not talking about merely observing a national holiday; we're talking about public sorrow that continued for hundreds of years.

Another way Jews would have understood mourning involved the grieving of corporate sin. Because community was so important to the Jewish identity, people understood that sin was not an isolated event.

They found it important to recognize individual participation in community injustice. Take Joel, for instance. He was an Old Testament prophet who went to great lengths to mourn over—and repent for—Israel when the nation turned its back on God. Joel's sorrow wasn't a result of his sin alone but of the sin of his entire nation.

Sometimes we forget to carry out this part of the story—the part where the Church confesses we aren't so squeaky clean, the part where saints get their hands dirty by sharing in the blame—and the burden—of sorrow.

In our world today, as in ancient Israel, there are far too many opportunities for our hearts to be broken by our sin as well as others' sin. The rain falls on the just and the unjust. But that's not the final word. Christ promised to show us comfort so fully that we would then be able to turn around and comfort others (2 Cor. 1:3-4).

When Joel cried and anguished over the sins of the Israelites because he was a part of that sinful nation, he shared the blame. What does it mean to share the blame for community sin? Have you ever been a part of a group that did something wrong and you all took the blame? How does sharing the blame and working through it draw you into true community?

Talk

God promises to comfort those who mourn, no matter what we are mourning. Maybe you mourn for a friend far from God. Maybe you mourn because of sin in your own heart. Maybe you mourn because you feel the weight of someone else's pain and suffering. God wants to remind you that there will be comfort for us because he loves us that much. How has God shown comfort to you or someone you know?

# Going. Going. Gone.

Worship pastor Mike Crawford sings these words:

> "Blessed when plans
> that you so carefully laid
> end up in the junkyard with
> all the trash you made."[2]

Consider yourself and those you know who mourn the loss of broken dreams or futures that will never happen. Spend a week considering how God redeems the dreams and futures of those he loves.

**God redeems my dreams when . . .**

**My future is secure in Christ because . . .**

# 99 balloons closer to the kingdom.

Watch the video "99 Balloons" on youtube.com. Consider how a child's short ninety-nine days of life drew a community together in mourning. Think about how the kingdom of God came to the parents, to the friends of the family, to the child through those who shared both the joy and the grief of young Eliot's life.

Share the burden of mourning by getting a helium-filled balloon and letting it go for those who are mourning. If you are mourning, let it go as a symbol of the promise that God will comfort you.

**Journal your thoughts here.**

# A panoramic view.

Entire nations can lose their identities through war, exile, genocide, or poverty. Piled on top of personal loss is the loss of cultural and corporate identity. Go to tinyurl.com/cxljo8. View the University of Heidelberg's *Global Conflict Panorama*. Choose one of those areas to learn more about. Pray for those who are mourning in that situation.

**Journal your thoughts here.**

# An internal war.

Those who serve in our country's armed forces are at a high risk of depression and suicide. Provide comfort to them by sending them a letter, package, or card this week.

Go to: anysoldier.com/wheretosend.

Be sure to look closely at the "what to send" and "how to send" tabs to make sure your letter or package gets to a soldier needing comfort.

**Journal your thoughts here.**

**39**

# Wanna see someone's face light up?

Attend a hospital visitation with your pastor or youth pastor.

**Journal your thoughts here.**

40

_____

_____

_____

_____

# Remember life before singing animation and e-cards?

Handwrite a letter to someone in your life who is struggling with a hopeless or depressing situation. Text a prayer to them or give them a phone call this week. Listen to their story and do your best to encourage them. Try to keep in mind that God will be doing a lot of comforting through you; it's by Christ that you can do all things (Phil. 4:13).

**Journal your thoughts here.**

# Make a list.

Ask three people what sins they feel are the most prevalent in our nation's teen population. Then spend your quiet time this week allowing God to break your heart for those sins.

Maybe you've been a part of a sin that seems to be a struggle for a lot of people you know. Ask God to free you from its hold on your life and to help you reach out to those who struggle with the same thing.

**Journal your thoughts here.**

# Community options.

**1** Put a map in your youth room or small group location highlighting the area that you've chosen (tinyurl.com/cxljo8). Set up a prayer station for students to use each week. Allow for written prayers and recorded prayers using a laptop. Compile the prayers and send them to a Christian church in that same area.

**2** Feeling extra passionate? Get a group of friends to adopt someone who is hospital bound. Make sure your adopted friend receives something (a card, letter, flowers, candy, a phone call, etc.) every day for a week, a month, or for however long they need to be in the hospital. It's up to you.

**3** Create a Wailing Wall for prayer notes or sticky notes. The notes can be prayers for the forgiveness of sin or prayers for those who need great comfort and support.

# Blessed are the meek

"Blessed are the meek, for they will inherit the earth" (Matt. 5:5).

He was God's chosen leader for the entire Israelite nation. He split a sea in two. He called down boatloads of plagues. He got sassy with Pharaoh. And, "Moses was very meek . . . above all the men on the face of the earth" (Num. 12:3, AMP).

Wait, what?

If we are honest with ourselves, it seems unlikely that this man would be one of the Bible's foremost examples of meekness. In fact, isn't it natural to correlate meekness with someone timid? Maybe we've got the wrong idea about this whole meek thing.

Our understanding of meek comes from the Greek word *praus*, which is used to describe a broken colt, a gentle breeze, and soothing medicine.

If you look carefully at these definitions, they all have something in common. Mainly behind the gentleness [of the colt, wind, and medicine], there is strength under control.[3] This can apply to our humanity as well. Each of us represents a strong will, which can be used in one of two ways—either to lead people toward the kingdom or to drive them from it. In effect, God invites us all to become like Moses to the people around us.

One more thing: Jesus' statement that the meek will inherit the earth would have created lots of hope for the people hearing his message because it reminded them of the Jewish exodus. If you remember correctly, God had made this same promise to the lowly Israelites, saying they would inherit the earth . . . or what they called the Promised Land.

Jesus promised an inheritance for those who humbly follow God's lead. The Israelites didn't need to raise even a finger against the Egyptians when God delivered them.

True meekness is a difficult virtue to grab hold of. It's becoming both servant and leader. It's recognizing those who are overlooked and serving those on the edges.

Talk

Knowing Moses was described as "the meekest of all people on earth" may change what you have always thought of as meekness. After all, he did kill an Egyptian soldier, argue with God, and smash the Ten Commandments in a fit of rage. So how does this change your understanding of what meekness really means?

In a society constantly in pursuit of success, does meekness get in the way of succeeding? Can a person be driven and meek at the same time?

Share some examples of a meek person who has succeeded big time.

# Grin and bear it, whatever that means.

Everyone may deserve to be yelled at a little—especially when they are YELLING AT YOU. But this week, when you want to raise your voice, work to be gentle and soft-spoken instead.

**Journal your thoughts here.**

# Serving the snot-nosed.

Okay, admit it. You were a pain in the neck to all your grade school teachers. But some of those teachers still stand out in your memory as being outstanding. Write a letter to one, thanking him or her for being significant in your life.

# While you were sleeping. (This is not a shout-out to '90s chick flicks.)

Most churches have a cleaning/maintenance person or crew who works odd hours to keep the place in shape for you and other people who use the building. Theirs is an important and often overlooked ministry. Make some cookies this week, bring a snack, write a card–do something to show your appreciation for what they do when no one else is looking.

**Journal your thoughts here.**

# Mow and go.

Wait until they are gone, then mow your neighbor's yard. Don't let them know it was you.

If you don't have a mower (or a neighbor with a yard needing mowed), try washing someone's car instead. It's always okay to ask permission first.

(Be careful around lawn equipment. Get an adult to help you with this one.)

**Journal your thoughts here.**

# Dodgeball.

Choose the least likely players first for your dodgeball or kickball team in gym this month. Allow modesty and a gentle spirit to help you reach out to those who often get overlooked. Doing this will say, "You're just as important as I am."

**Journal your thoughts here.**

# Social network pick-me-up. (Which is better than the alternative: a social network throw-you-down.)

Using your social network of choice, publicly praise someone else at least once a day. Better yet, praise someone toward whom you feel competitive or jealous.

**Journal your thoughts here.**

# We're giving you permission to toot your own horn.

What is your gift? Are you a brilliant guitarist? Do you play the piano like Mozart? Are you a brainiac in English class? Whatever it is, offer your talents to help someone else—with no strings attached.

**Journal your thoughts here.**

# Community options.

1  As a group, have a church cleanup day. Help with yard work around the church property or with the weekly cleaning responsibility. Try to do the work anonymously.

2  In our youth groups, some people just naturally get run over because they don't have the same big mouths the rest of us have. Maybe it's the youngest or the newest members. Think about who those people are and throw them a party. Let them know you appreciate them.

# Blessed
# are those
# who hunger
# and thirst

"Blessed are those who hunger and thirst
for righteousness, for they will be
filled" (Matt. 5:6).

For several centuries, our Western culture has been on a path of affluence. Because we are able to meet most every want and need that arises, we automatically assume life owes us not only the basics but the luxuries as well.

We're comfortable, even during hard economic times. So the idea of an urgent, life-threatening need can be distant for many of us.

But you've got to remember that the Sermon on the Mount was given at a different time, to a different people. And when Jesus (being a thoughtful orator) wanted to flesh out the idea of desperation, he had to make it relevant to his audience.

Their response would have been, *Yeah, desert thirst and empty bellies for forty years. We get that.*

He's telling us to be so desperate for righteousness that our existence depends on it.

That word, righteousness, is a difficult word to understand. That's because we have strayed away from its original meaning, which in the biblical story was translated more closely to *divine justice*.[4] For the Jews, empire oppression meant many were forced to give up their land and sell themselves or their family members into slavery.

But that wasn't supposed to be the end of the story. There was always the communal hope of things being put right. God wanted to put some skin on what righteousness looked like. And so the law stated that at the end of every forty-nine years, people should experience restoration. Every slave freed. All land returned. Inheritances restored. Debts forgiven.

They called this the year of Jubilee.

**57**

Yet there is no evidence that Jubilee was ever practiced in Israel even though it was in their law. Guess they never quite brought themselves around to doing it though the ideals were nice enough. Which begs the question, why was it so difficult for Jubilee to happen then . . . and now?

do not depend on the hope
of results. you may have
to face the fact that your
work will be apparently
**worthless** and even
achieve no result at all, if not
perhaps results opposite to what
you expect. as you get used to this
idea, you start more and more to
concentrate not on the results, but
on the value, the rightness, the
truth of the work itself.

**Thomas Merton**

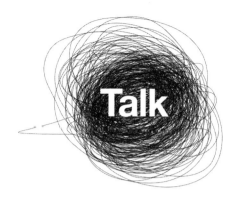

Talk

What do you think the reaction would be if Jubilee became a law in the United States? All things returning to their rightful owners. All debts wiped clean. All houses with mortgages paid off. Would it be well received? What problems would arise?

Jesus came to announce the kingdom of God with his arrival. How does Jesus proclaim a spiritual jubilee in our hearts? How do you think we are to respond to kingdom ideals (blessed are the poor, etc.), especially knowing Jesus proclaimed this when he was on earth (Luke 4:18-21)?

So we may not have a Jubilee year, but Jesus opened up a Jubilee age where the kingdom of God breaks in and we are able to experience a new order and way to live. How can we show true righteousness in our current kingdom age?

# Silence is golden. (And we've got a hunch that both silence and gold are equally rare.)

In order to go after righteousness, some have found it necessary to remove themselves from the mainstream. Even Jesus drew back and isolated himself as a way to gather strength (you see him do this at the most intense times of his ministry). Take time away from your busy life. Spend a night alone in your room or a few hours in a place that is sacred to you (a park, a bench, perhaps an altar at church). Limit your external distractions (turn off your phone and leave the video game and iPod alone) so you can spend time in reflection and meditation.

**Journal your thoughts here.**

# The big Book.
# Enough said.

Commit to reading three chapters in the Bible this week (try Matthew 5, 6, and 7). Read the chapters expecting God to teach you something.

**Journal your thoughts here.**

# Please doodle.

For one month, take notes on your pastor's sermons as a way to make sure you are paying attention to God's word for you. Even better, try to make what you learned a part of your life.

**Journal your thoughts here.**

# Justice at town hall.

Jubilee may not exist in your hometown, but that doesn't mean you can't play an active role in the redemption of your community. Learn what issues are facing your local community council or parent teacher association.

**Journal your thoughts here.**

# Be desperate.
# For God.

Righteousness is being desperate for God and depending on him. What are some other things you choose to depend on rather than God? Make a list of things you tend to depend on; then ask God for strength and wisdom to depend on God instead of these things.

**Journal your thoughts here.**

# That cardigan is, like, so cute and slave-free.

A personal relationship with Jesus should have a direct effect on social action. Often the things we buy, whether we know it or not, help support slavery in other countries.

This week, visit chainstorereaction.com and send an e-mail to one of the stores asking them to do their part in ending slavery.

**Journal your thoughts here.**

# The price is right?

When you choose to draw near to God and to hunger and thirst for righteousness, there is a price. That price is a longing to make things right. Not only will you want to make things right in your heart before a loving God, but you will also want to make things right with people in your life. Make something right this week. Ask a friend for forgiveness, get over that grudge, seek out a compromise with your parents on that thing that's been standing between you. Whatever it is, make it right.

**Journal your thoughts here.**

# Community options.

**1** Take a Bible-reading journey as a group. For further direction, see Biblein90days.com. You could even kick the ninety days off with an overnighter where everyone takes turns reading a portion of the Bible out loud.

**2** Host a group barbecue. Allow everyone to create a list of his or her own obstacles to righteousness. Insert the lists into a charcoal chimney starter and use them as fuel to ignite the coals. Consider the experience a commitment to letting go of those things we come to depend on.

Make sure an adult is present during this experiment and in charge of the fire. It's always a good idea to have a fire extinguisher on hand . . . just in case.

**3** Pick one store on the site chainstorereaction.com and have each person in the group write an e-mail to them. Make an intentional effort to get one store to respond to the call to have slave-free practices.

# Blessed are the merciful

"Blessed are the merciful, for they will be shown mercy" (Matt. 5:7).

One way we can figure out what's important to people is to listen to what they say and notice when they repeat things. These repetitions are clues to what lies in their hearts. So when Matthew tells us three times that Jesus insisted on us being merciful (5:7, 9:13, 12:7), we can pretty much bank on it being core to his message.

The Jews would have recognized immediately that Matthew's comments on mercy were actually quotes from the book of Hosea. "For I desire mercy, not sacrifice" (6:6a).[5] From where we stand, it sounds logical that God would prefer forgiveness over ritualistic animal slaughter. I mean, what a bloody mess. But Jesus was emphasizing something pretty huge. By suggesting that mercy was more important than giving a sacrifice—the greatest forgiveness offering in the Old Testament—he was challenging a well-established system of religion.

What it comes down to is this: God's greatest desire for us is to copy the mercy he has shown us. But he's the polite sort, not likely to force his way on us. Rather, he invites us into a way of mercy. The choice is ours. And if we do not feel that compassion and forgiveness are the better way to live, well there's just no way we can expect to receive them. Judge and be judged.

Remember the story of the king who cancelled his servant's huge debt, only to have that servant turn around and imprison his friend over pocket change (Matt. 18:33)? Apparently he didn't get the memo.

The true follower of God mimics the actions of Jesus. A follower is transformed when he or she receives mercy, making it then a natural response to show mercy toward others. That's why it's a good thing we have the perfect example of mercy in Jesus himself. It doesn't get any better than a messed up sinner being shown mercy by God. And unless our righteousness surpasses that of the Pharisees (Matt. 5:20), we need God's mercy because the good things we do will never be enough to win his favor.

**Talk**

Jesus says we will be blessed if we are merciful. But being merciful isn't always easy, especially with people who don't deserve it. In what

situation do you find it hardest to show mercy? What makes it so difficult?

The call to be merciful can also be a challenge to those already opening their hearts to God. What are some ways to be open to acts of mercy God may be calling you to participate in?

# Let the moocher live.

We all know a moocher or someone who owes us. Forgive their debt, big or small, and forget about it. And by that, we mean don't tell them.

**Journal your thoughts here.**

# No whining: a variation of the Golden Rule.

Think of some pet peeves you have based on what others do. Recognize that you have your own behaviors that drive others crazy. And because you know this, make room for others' quirks by refusing to whine about them.

**Journal your thoughts here.**

# Hot food is overrated anyway.

We've all had waiters or waitresses who forgot our drinks and then vanished for twenty minutes only to bring out cold food and a tomato on what was supposed to be a plain cheeseburger. Maybe he or she was having a bad day. Use some of your money to give a bad restaurant server a good tip this week just because you know mercy is a good thing.

**Journal your thoughts here.**

# What stop sign?

Wouldn't it be great if someone else paid for our mistakes? Exactly. Collect loose change in your group or on your own and give it to an adult to pay someone's traffic fine. Christ paid a price for us that we didn't deserve. Practice this and be grateful.

**Journal your thoughts here.**

# Maybe a box. Maybe a mansion . . . doesn't matter.

It's easy to become skeptical of beggars on street corners. This month, don't think about how they became homeless. Just show mercy by going to a local homeless outreach that feeds those who are hungry. Smile and look for the stories behind the eyes.

**Journal your thoughts here.**

# Ugh, I *would* get stuck behind a student driver.

Hurry often short-circuits our ability to be patient. Lack of patience then leads to a lack of compassion when others force us to slow down. This week, if you can drive, do some spiritual training in patience—drive to and from school and work (or any errand) without passing anyone. And just in case you were thinking of tailgating grandma to urge her along, don't.

If you can't drive yet, talk to the person who does most of the driving for you about doing this. They may think you're crazy . . . but people thought Jesus was crazy too.

**Journal your thoughts here.**

# We'll call him "the frenemy." (Yeah, that's not a real word.)

Completely unaware of other people's feelings. Dominates conversation. Throws you under the bus. Can never admit to being wrong. We all have a friend who tries our patience or has betrayed our trust. Rise above the frustration. Be the friend you wish he or she could be, and don't hold a grudge if that friend doesn't seem to change.

**Journal your thoughts here.**

# Community options.

1 There's a person in your church whose faith is dying because they can't pay a bill or meet their family's needs. Acknowledge the need and show mercy by helping to meet that need together, anonymously.

2 Go together as a group to support a homeless outreach or mission. Do whatever it takes to serve, even if it means giving up a Saturday.

83

# Blessed are the pure in heart

"Blessed are the pure in heart, for they will see God" (Matt. 5:8).

You've heard it before. And often.

*I love you with all my heart.*

*You broke my heart.*

*Invite Jesus into your heart.*

We know that no one is literally talking about the beating muscle between our rib bones. How very unsentimental. Rather, the heart is considered the core of a person's devotion, love, strength, and faith. At least, that's what Hallmark says.

What's important to recognize is that when Jesus blessed those who are pure in heart, he was being kind of counter cultural.

Don't get me wrong, the priests in biblical times were known for being sticklers where purity was concerned. But it just so happened that the laws of outward purity were the only ones anyone seemed to care much about. The Jews had rules addressing how many times to wash your hands in a given day, what kinds of food were pure, and whom you couldn't touch. And yet these laws of cleanliness failed to address the most important

cleansing of all—the cleansing of human will and devotion—the cleansing of the heart.

Jesus was doing a new thing. And it was messing with people who were deeply rooted in religious piety. In fact, the Pharisees thought Jesus embodied a sort of unreligion due to his association with the impure of society (Luke 7:34).

During the Sermon on the Mount, Christ made it clear that belief meant spiritual transformation, not just routine-following. No longer was being pure only about abstaining from murder or deception but refraining from nasty thoughts as well. All of a sudden, lustful thoughts were being compared to adultery.

**85**

Seems like we are set up for failure. Yet in saying all this, Jesus was pointing to the fact that people cannot, in themselves, become pure. God instead desires to do this good work in us, through relationship.

The choice to be pure in heart becomes a matter of allowing him to change us so we can see him in the world around us.

he that but looketh
on a plate of
ham and eggs
to **lust** after
it hath already
committed
breakfast with it in
his heart.

C.S. Lewis

Jewish laws stated many specifics about outward cleanliness but avoided specifics on the cleanliness of the heart. Why do you think they focused on the outward rules so much more than we do today?

Talk

Jesus says the pure in heart will see God. Assuming this does not mean a repeat of the burning bush, in what ways do you believe God shows himself to you when you strive to have a pure heart?

89

# Media fast . . . and by that we don't mean get *faster* at flipping through channels.

Unplug from all media activity for a week as a means to simplify your life. Instead of watching TV, surfing the Internet, or playing with a game system, spend some time outside. Seek God and *listen*.

90 **Journal your thoughts here.**

# Bring a lighter.

Visit your church when nobody is there. (Ask for permission first.) Pray in silence for the people of your community. Pray for others' struggles and addictions as well as your own. Light a candle to symbolize each person you raised up in prayer. Try tea lights. Don't forget to blow them out when you're finished.

**Journal your thoughts here.**

# XXX

# For your protection.

Sign up for the accountability program at xxxchurch.com. It doesn't matter if you have ever struggled with an Internet addiction or not. This is a safeguard against future temptation.

Xxxchurch will keep you accountable to having a pure heart when on the computer.

**Journal your thoughts here.**

# It's called an alarm clock. (Or the evil offspring of technology.)

Carve out space every morning to memorize Ps. 139:23-24. Pray the verses for a week (or month), asking God to reveal those areas of your life that act as a block in your relationship with him.

# I get by with a little help from my friends.

If you don't already have an accountability partner, seek out a trusted friend and set up times to meet regularly. Use these times to share joys, struggles, temptations, and everyday life. One of the main reasons God created the body of Christ was so we could encourage and support one another through this faith journey.

**Journal your thoughts here.**

# Go green. (That is, if you're a real straggler and haven't jumped on the bandwagon yet.)

Purity doesn't stop at the physical boundaries we set for ourselves. It also involves how we treat our bodies and the earth around us. You may love your bag of Cheetos, but for one week eat fresh foods. (And not because it's trendy.) Refill a reusable water bottle instead of wasting plastic disposable bottles. See that purity comes in all shapes and sizes.

**Journal your thoughts here.**

# Wait training.

Make a commitment to things that will keep you physically pure in your relationships. Group dates. Keeping the doors open. Avoiding dark places. Staying rooted in God's Word and in prayer.

God designed us for sex inside the covenant of a lifelong relationship. Mark this date (if you haven't already) as the day you begin your "wait training" and commit to saving sex for one amazing person.

**Journal your thoughts here.**

# Community options.

1 Take your media fast one step further: examine your media choices individually. Write down those choices you would like to avoid or eliminate in order to dedicate yourself to purity. Give these choices to an accountability partner or youth leader.

2 Take a candle to people your group prayed for this week. Include a note explaining that you lifted them up in prayer.

3 Have a commitment service for those wanting to start "wait training." Provide something for each student to help them remember their commitment on a daily basis.

# Blessed are the peacemakers

"Blessed are the peacemakers, for they will be called the sons of God" (Matt. 5:9).

Could be your spirit kind of recoils at the sound of conflict. Could be you have tried to act as the mediator between friends, parents, or siblings. That is, until you got hurt. Until you stepped in between a proverbial war of words, or a not-so-proverbial fistfight. That's one black eye comin' up.

Could be that now you've learned some survival skills. And at the sound of slammed doors and raised voices, you retreat to a neutral corner. You still desire peace; you just stopped pursuing it. Which, more plainly put, means giving in to doing nothing.

When Jesus said blessed are the peacemakers, he was being intentional about his language. Notice he didn't say *peacelovers*. He was asking us to be participants in the work of restoration. To leave our couches. To keep the powers of darkness from having a field day. To actively pursue peace until a new and better kingdom is realized.

Even so, waiting for such a kingdom is hard. It's easy to feel despair at the prospect of never reaching peace in the world, and Jesus' words aren't all that comforting. "You will hear of wars and rumors of wars, but see to it that you are not alarmed. Such things must happen, but the end is still to come" (Matt. 24:6).

It feels like we're just running around in circles. So then, is there something to be done?

Yes. Especially if our view of peace extends beyond what we have generally thought it to be. Peace, or the Hebrew word, *shalom*, means something more profound than just the absence of conflict. More appropriately, this word was used in the Bible to represent completeness or wholeness.[6] Jesus' listeners would have known this to include total reconciliation with God, neighbor, and nations.

**99**

Isaiah 61 mentions a whole slew of ways peace can be made—releasing prisoners, binding up broken hearts, bestowing beauty. Notice that force and fear are not the catalysts for God's shalom. So what does actively working to achieve peace look like for us today?

Would you describe yourself as more of a peacelover, a peacemaker, or neither? What do you think caused you to be the way you are?

Talk

If peace is more than just the absence of conflict, what can we do to be active peacemakers?

# Not a Grammy. Or an Oscar. But they do alright for themselves.

If you have trouble believing that peacemakers still exist, do some research on men and women who have received the Nobel Peace Prize. Pick one or two and reflect on the way they used their gifts to improve our lives. How can you create peace with your talents?

**Journal your thoughts here.**

# Bite your tongue. (Eeewww you're bleeding; that's not what we meant.)

The Scriptures say it's a pretty good idea to be "quick to listen and slow to speak" (James 1:19). But as reactionary creatures, this is hard for us. This week hold your tongue in arguments, even when you think you are in the right. Once you have listened, calmed down, and prayed about your response, then speak your mind. Be the active peacemaker in a conflict.

**Journal your thoughts here.**

# Give a hug.

Sometimes peace is as simple as giving a friend a hug. Give a hug this week. In fact, give a few. Hugs are free.

# Little books, big thoughts. (Okay, okay, we really just like the pictures.)

Todd Parr (a children's author) wrote *The Peace Book*, a book about the different ways peace can be made in our world. Buy a copy or check one out at the library and keep it with you. Try peace in your own way. If your little brother or sister owns this book, ask before borrowing it (to keep the peace).

**Journal your thoughts here.**

# We actually *like* crayons on the wall—saves us the wallpaper hassle.

Chaos is a word most people add to their vocabulary after having children. While endearing, children aren't known as the most peaceful of all beings. Create peace in someone's life by offering to babysit while they go out for the night. Another option is to volunteer in your children's ministry on Sunday. Maybe some of the regulars would like to hear a sermon every once in a while.

**Journal your thoughts here.**

# The good. The badge. And the ugly.

Consider people in your town who play active roles in peacemaking: police, teachers, civil servants, pastors. Write them a letter of affirmation, make a donation, or prepare something special to show your appreciation.

**Journal your thoughts here.**

# Zebras.

Referees are the peacemakers on the field, but seldom do they receive anything but verbal assaults. Doesn't matter if it was a ball or strike, foul or pick, first down or turnover. Keep your complaints to yourself, and personally thank the refs when the game has ended.

**Journal your thoughts here.**

# Community options.

1  Make up your own group "peace prize." Name it something fun and give it to someone you know who is really great at being a role model of peace. Maybe it's a teacher who is great at helping students see different points of views or a friend who doesn't get angry very easily. Make the prize out of whatever you like and let them know you appreciate their peaceful ways.

2  Plan a free babysitting night at the church so parents have the opportunity to take a night off in peace. Make sure you have at least one adult there to help supervise.

3  As a group, write a letter or take a snack over to your local fire station, police station, or to another group of peacemakers. When you take the gift, make sure to tell them how much you appreciate what they do for the community.

# Blessed are those who are persecuted

"Blessed are those who are persecuted because of righteousness, for theirs is the kingdom of heaven" (Matt. 5:10 ).

Jesus opened and closed his conversation on the Beatitudes by reminding us that our hope is in the age to come.

When we look closely, we see that things on earth are not as they were intended to be. The world feels broken. And there is no greater proof of this brokenness than the persecution of saints.

It's humbling to know that Christians continue to face hostility in many places worldwide. It happens so often that there is an entire news service—compassdirect.org—established just to report it all. However, Jesus assured his followers that their persecution and martyrdom would not be in vain. "I tell you the truth, unless a kernel of wheat falls to the ground and dies, it remains only a single seed. But if it dies, it produces many seeds" (John 12:24).

Christianity began in the tough places and still thrives there. In fact, the areas of the world where believers receive the strongest resistance are the areas where the church seems to be growing the most.

So why would persecution promote growth? Maybe because the kingdom is bigger than a generic morality that people don't agree with, such as a political stance. Maybe it's more like a movement that incites others to respond. Maybe the kingdom is a real threat to the establishments, and that gets people excited. Maybe if we are living the kingdom life, our righteousness will publicly be at odds with our present culture.

Like we said, Jesus ended the Beatitudes the same way he began them: "for theirs is the kingdom of heaven." The journey has come full circle. The poor and the persecuted (and everyone in between) have something in common: they are hopeless to find relief in this present world. After all, society can't offer much in the way of comfort when we are living contrary to its patterns. And isn't that so like God, to obliterate our presuppositions and replace them with new paradigms? The kingdom is backwards. But it is setting us free.

something is **wrong** when our lives make sense to unbelievers.

Francis Chan

**Talk**

How does living the kingdom make us at odds with the current culture? What does it feel like to stand up for those who are persecuted or shunned?

Many Christians around the world are persecuted because of their beliefs, but are there groups the Church persecutes? What groups of people does the church shun or turn away from? What can we do to reach out to these people?

# Pray for the persecuted.

The Web site opendoorsusa.org has a World Watch List that continually reports which countries suffer the greatest persecution for their religious beliefs. Download the list and pray for a different area each night.

**Journal your thoughts here.**

# Voice of the Martyrs.

The Voice of the Martyrs is a nonprofit group that strives to make the world aware of the persecution Christians suffer. Go to their Web site at be-a-voice.net. Become a part of the Be-A-Voice network, then find the profile of a persecuted Christian and make a commitment to write to and pray for this person.

**Journal your thoughts here.**

# You have 346,918 Facebook friends. (Give or take a few.)

But not everyone is a social whiz. In your youth group, there are people who are lonely—outcasts either by intentional or unintentional exclusion. Find someone like this and become involved in his or her life. Sit with that person at lunch. Invite him or her to be a part of your small group or to be a part of an activity outside of church.

**Journal your thoughts here.**

# Open lunch.

Chances are, you sit with the same crew every day for lunch. Make some room at your table and invite someone lonely to join you. And don't just let them sit there awkwardly by themselves. Get to know her, learn his story, show mercy . . . this whole kingdom thing is coming together.

**Journal your thoughts here.**

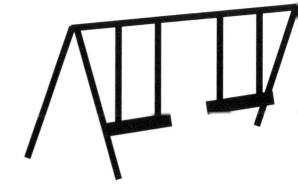

# Lots of bullies on the playground.

More Christians have been persecuted in the last hundred years than in all of the previous nineteen hundred years since the time of Christ. You might be surprised to know of persecution against Christians that happens close to home. Go to christianfreedom.org and search under United States, Mexico, or UK to inform yourself about persecution near you.

**Journal your thoughts here.**

# IDOP. (You're thinking about pancakes right now, aren't you?)

Well, we are talking about something altogether different. Visit persecutedchurch.org and order a free IDOP (International Day of Prayer) kit. Use it to make your church or youth group aware of the needs of persecuted Christians around the world.

**Journal your thoughts here.**

**121**

# Parent pain.

We live in a world where many teenagers have taken their own lives or the lives of others while being reckless, depressed, or irresponsible. Tragedies happen, and oftentimes the parents are left hurting with feelings of guilt and loneliness. Send flowers or words of encouragement to a family in your community that is hurting from a pain from the past. It could have been last week or ten years ago. The pain of loss never goes away. Don't judge. Simply show love to those who have experienced great pain in their lives.

# Community options.

1  As a group, commit to pray for the persecuted Christians around the world. Sign up for weekly Prayer Bulletin e-mails from opendoorsusa.org. Print out these bulletins for everyone in the group—and pass them out to others and encourage them to pray as well.

2  Listen to the song "Lost Get Found" by Britt Nicole. Print out the lyrics and talk about how you can "not let the fire burn out" as a group. Talk about how the lost get found by the way you live your lives together. Talk about the easy road and the ways you tend to play it safe. Then challenge each other to take chances for God together.

Go one step further: have each student put this song on their mp3 players. Let the song be an anthem for your group for a week, a month, a semester, whatever it takes.

# Endnotes

1 Roger L. Hahn, *Matthew: A Commentary for Bible Students* (Indianapolis: Wesleyan Publishing House, 2007), 103.

2 Mike Crawford and his Secret Siblings, *Songs from Jacob's Well*, vol. 2, "Words to Build a Life on" (2008).

3 William Barclay, *New Testament Words* (Louisville, KY: Westminster John Knox Press 2000), 241.

4 Michael J. Wilkins, *The NIV Application Commentary* (Grand Rapids: Zondervan Publishing, 2004), 207.

5 Roger L. Hahn, Matthew: *A Commentary for Bible Students*, 103.

6 Michael J. Wilkins, *The NIV Application Commentary*, 209.

# Notes:

# Notes:

Copyright 2010
by The House Studio

ISBN 978-0-8341-2516-2

Printed in the
United States of America

Cover and Interior Design by J.R. Caines and Arthur Cherry
Photography by Arthur Cherry

10  9  8  7  6  5  4  3

the kingdom is backwards